Fun on the Track

Written by Emily Hooton

Collins

Go-karts are terrific! Get set to zoom!

flag

kart

track

helmet

belt

Put on a helmet and strap the belt tight.

4

6

Press down hard. Go!

Tuck arms in tight. The karts might bump and crash!

This kart turns left at the bend. If you turn too hard, you might crash the kart!

11

Karts dart to get by. They slam into the rails.

13

Bang! This kart is smashed from the back.
It spins and thumps the kerb hard.

15

The finish is in sight. The quickest is the winner today!

Go-kart blog

At the weekend, I went karting with my sister. It was terrific!

I was winning! Then a kart rammed into me and I crashed. My sister darted by, but her kart got stuck. I dashed to the flag to win!

Zoom to win

bump

bend

20

sprint

spin

21

At the track

 Review: After reading

Use your assessment from hearing the children read to choose any GPCs, words or tricky words that need additional practice.

Read 1: Decoding

- Talk about the meaning of the phrases below in the context of go-kart racing. Ask: How would you explain this to someone?
  - page 13 – **sprint off** (*speed away/accelerate*)
  - page 15 – **get level** (*be alongside the other racers/catch up*)
- Focus on words with adjacent consonants and short vowels. How quickly can the children read these words accurately?

track	**smashed**	**rest**	**karting**
slam	**thumps**	**next**	**crashed**

Read 2: Prosody

- Model reading page 12 in the excited voice of a live sports broadcaster, then model reading page 13 as an authoritative and encouraging instructor. Can the children hear the difference?
- Ask the children, working in pairs, to take it in turns to read each page in the appropriate voice.
- Remind them to emphasise the important and exciting words when reading (e.g. **dart**, **slam**).
- Bonus content: Focus on pages 18 and 19, and tell the children which words you would emphasise to create excitement. Give them choices on how to say the verbs: **winning**, **rammed**, **crashed**.

Read 3: Comprehension

- Ask the children if they have ever seen a go-kart race or whether they have been on a go-kart. Discuss whether they would find it exciting to drive a go-kart, and why.
- Ask: Do you think this is a useful book for someone who is going to race a go-kart? Why? Focus on the pages featuring the instructors and what they teach.
- Challenge the children to explain the karting day using the pictures on pages 22 and 23.
- Read out the following statements and ask: Is this true or false? Why? You could give the page numbers to help them.
  - Pages 4 and 5: The only thing you need before setting off is a strap. (*false* – **Put on a helmet**)
  - Pages 8 and 9: The go-karts line up at the start line. (*false* – **The karts zoom off from the grid**)
  - Pages 10 and 11: Turning a bend takes a lot of skill. (*true* – **If you turn too hard, you might crash the kart!**)